A QUICK GUIDE TO
Teaching Informational Writing
Grade 2

MARIKA PÁEZ WIESEN

Workshop Help Desk Series
Edited by Lucy Calkins
with the Reading and Writing Project

DEDICATED TO TEACHERS™
HEINEMANN
Portsmouth, NH

An imprint of Heinemann
361 Hanover Street
Portsmouth, NH 03801–3912
www.heinemann.com

Offices and agents throughout the world

Library of Congress Cataloging-in-Publication Data
Wiesen, Marika Páez.
  A quick guide to teaching informational writing, grade 2 / Marika Páez Wiesen.
     p. cm. — (Workshop help desk series)
  Includes bibliographical references.
  ISBN-13: 978-0-325-02690-9
  ISBN-10: 0-325-02690-4
  1. English language—Composition and exercises—Study and teaching (Primary).
  2. Exposition (Rhetoric)—Study and teaching (Primary). I. Title.
  LB1528.W5 2012
  372.62'3—dc23   2011032915

SERIES EDITOR: *Lucy Calkins* and the *Reading and Writing Project*
EDITORS: *Kate Montgomery* and *Teva Blair*
PRODUCTION: *Victoria Merecki*
COVER DESIGN: *Monica Crigler* and *Jenny Jensen Greenleaf*
COVER PHOTO: *Peter Cunningham, www.petercunninghamphotography.com*
INTERIOR DESIGN: *Jenny Jensen Greenleaf*
COMPOSITION: *House of Equations, Inc.*
MANUFACTURING: *Veronica Bennett*

Printed in the United States of America on acid-free paper
16 15 14 13 12 VP 1 2 3 4 5

For the ever-supportive,
very missed Ann . . .
"Hooray!"

C O N T E N T S

ACKNOWLEDGMENTS

John Muir once said, "When we try to pick out anything by itself, we find it hitched to everything else in the Universe." This book is no exception. It is, indeed, hitched to many, many people in this universe. First and foremost, I'd like to thank Lucy Calkins for her keen vision and generous mentorship in this project. You have been a giant upon whose shoulders I have been incredibly privileged to stand. And to all of my colleagues at the Reading and Writing Project—I am so grateful to all of you for your passion, generosity, kindness, and brilliance. Thanks especially to Laurie Pessah, Kathleen Tolan, Mary Ehrenworth, Kathy Collins, Shanna Schwartz, Amanda Hartman, Sarah Picard Taylor, Beth Moore, and Gravity Goldberg. Warm thanks goes to Jen Serravallo; I never could have gotten started without you. And a big thank you to Stacey Fell-Eisenkraft; I never could have finished without you! Thank you, thank you for your tireless cheerleading and editing. I am so grateful to Kate Montgomery and Teva Blair at Heinemann for their reading, rereading, suggesting, and believing! Thank you to all of the incredible teachers who thought with me and let me borrow their students and their work—especially Jill-Marie Mika, Maria Liz, Maureen Krawec, Teresa Nakouzi, and Kate Bishop. Thank you to Gianna Cassetta and Lucy Malka for being my first and hardest staff developers, pushing my teaching further than I ever thought it could go. To the writers in my writing group—Jane Dougherty, Heidi Siegel, and Alison Gardiner—thanks for your encouragement through the *many* ups and downs! Thank you to all of my family for always rooting me on and giving me courage. And finally, thank you to Eric—husband, editor, heart's friend. I love you.

"Miss Marika! Miss Marika! Did you know . . . ?"

Day after day in my second-grade classroom, the air was filled with these outbursts—students tugging my arm, waving their hands wildly in the air, dying to share the new and strange discoveries that were rocking their world on a daily basis.

"Did you know that the sun is a *star*?"

"My aunt had a baby, and she let me hold it, and after you feed it you have to burp it like this . . . but sometimes it throws up on you."

"Did you know that a tomato is really a *fruit*?"

"My dad bought me a new game and it has fifteen levels. I finally figured out how to beat the guy on level eight and now I'm on level nine."

Informational writing is a genre that takes many forms. In many classrooms, it is known as report writing. The Common Core State Standards refer to it as informational or explanatory writing. By whichever name one uses, it is a perfect genre for second graders, for at its very heart is an insatiable desire to know more and to teach everyone around you everything you know. And nobody is more curious about the workings of the world, or more eager to tell you a zillion facts about the topic on hand, than a second grader. They seem to be hardwired to explore and wonder about all of the nooks and crannies in their own worlds and beyond, and then eagerly cram what they've found into back pockets and jelly jars to show off to everyone who'll listen.

While it's true that most second graders are dying to share and teach about their passions, as teachers we know it is also true that in a single classroom our writers' attitudes toward and experience with informational writing can vary a great deal. In my own classroom, one student's early obsession with dinosaurs led to reading stacks and stacks of dinosaur books, watching innumerable dinosaur documentaries, visiting several museum exhibits, and being encouraged to share and teach what he knew with every visiting relative. Meanwhile, on the other side of the spectrum were students whose previous exposure to informational texts had been mostly limited to a few school-based experiences.

Not only did my students vary in their experience with informational texts but they also varied in their confidence and fluency as writers. One student, Renee, struggled long and hard to write one or two sentences, while another, Evan, wrote pages and pages (and pages!). And many classrooms have more than one student like Arshdeep, who had arrived in the country just a few months ago and hadn't yet learned English.

In my work as a staff developer at the Reading and Writing Project, I had the opportunity to collaborate with many other RWP colleagues and with teachers, coaches, and principals as they sought to plan and implement informational writing units of study for classrooms filled with a wide range of learners. Many of the ideas in this book came out of those hours of professional collaboration.

The ideas in this book stand fundamentally on the shoulders of the thinking of all of my colleagues at the Reading and Writing Project, and especially build on the work described by Lucy Calkins and co-author Laurie Pessah in their book, *Nonfiction Writing: Procedures and Reports*, a part of the series *Units of Study for Primary Writing*. The ideas in that book have transformed primary writing workshops in New York City and across the country, and watching those ideas come to life in hundreds of classrooms has inspired me to imagine these next horizons.

My hope is that the ideas in this book will help teachers in yet other schools to plan instruction in informational writing in ways that make it closely attuned to second grade students' individual strengths and needs. This book aims to support teachers who work with a full spectrum of students, including those who come to school as avid researchers and writers as well as those for whom informational texts will feel like new terrain.

Ultimately, my hope is that this book will serve as a helpful road map, guiding our journey through the rich and wonderful terrain of informational writing. My hope is that teachers as well as students make the journey with a spirit of delight and wonder, returning with back pockets and jelly jars full.

CHAPTER ONE

Getting Ready

Planning and Preparing for Informational Writing Units That Fit Young Writers' Passions, Interests, and Abilities

When I was beginning my own foray into informational writing, my wonderfully nice teacher, Mrs. Dalpaghetto, made the awfully unwelcome announcement that the class would be writing reports. As you can guess, I did *not* like writing reports. Writing reports meant work—boring work. Namely, reading old, frayed books from the library that smelled like mildew, and then "putting it in your own words," as my teachers had reminded me over and over (which felt like a lot of silly work, since the author had chosen perfectly nice ones in the first place!).

This report, as it turned out, was a little different. We were asked to write a report about our families. As usual, I left the majority of my writing until the very last day before it was due, only to find that I was actually quite unhappy about not having even more time to work on it. As I pored over family pictures and considered everything I wanted to share, I got more and more excited about report writing. "Here is my chance," I thought to myself, "to interview my mom and finally get to the bottom of the mystery of what she really does all day while I'm stuck at school!" (Of course, interviewing and accurately synthesizing information are two different things! I ended up writing, "She likes to drive around all day and listen to country music," a gross distortion of fact if ever there was one!)

Writing that report about my family also gave me another opportunity—the opportunity to share myself. It was through writing that report that I first began trying to put into words how my family was different from other families I knew—my parents had separated that year, and my dad had moved to Southern California, hundreds of miles away.

I wouldn't say that the writing in that report was particularly good, but I do know that I worked harder and with more enthusiasm on that report than on any other I can remember. It's also one of the few pieces of "school-writing" that I've held onto, ensuring that it survived multiple cross-country moves.

Reflecting on my own writing experiences helps me remember that it's important to walk in our students' shoes a little when we begin planning for a unit of study. We know that our classrooms contain some students who feel reluctant to write at all, let alone write in an informational genre. We must carefully plan how we'll begin our unit to rally as much of our students' energy and enthusiasm as possible. We want them racing to the page (as I did that night), thinking, "Here's my chance to teach what I know and to find out more! I can't wait to get started!"

Once we've sparked that enthusiasm, we'll want to build on it while helping students develop the key writing skills and strategies they'll need to get stronger in writing any informational text. The Common Core State Standards have reminded us once again of the importance of this genre and the many forms this kind of writing can take. We know that in just one or two short years many of our students will sit in fourth- and fifth-grade classrooms where they'll be asked to read difficult nonfiction texts, "take notes," and then write a report "in their own words." Perhaps even more challenging, fourth and fifth graders are often asked to write essays in which they are ambitiously required to articulate ideas about a topic and then be able to develop and defend those ideas!

This chapter will help our second graders get off to a strong start toward meeting these ambitious goals. I'll outline a possible plan for the unit and then suggest a step-by-step support for getting started with the fundamental work that read-alouds and shared writing will play.

A Possible Plan for This Unit

My colleagues at the Reading and Writing Project have long suggested that students need many opportunities across the year to write informational texts. In most classrooms, teachers will want to plan *at least* two units of study in informational writing—along with the great deal of informational writing students are doing in science, social studies, math, and the arts, of course! Second-grade teachers will also want to plan a unit or two on opinion writing, a genre that not only incorporates loads of information but also has a structure similar to informational writing.

The first of these informational writing units might be called something like "All-About Books." In this first informational writing unit, students will most likely be writing about topics on which they have personal expertise, drawing on their experiences and knowledge. Later in the year, children will presumably undertake a second unit of study in informational writing, this time writing about a topic they've learned about through research. Many teachers provide yet a third informational writing unit, perhaps one that circles a whole-class shared topic. Readers may wonder why I'm suggesting a sequence that begins with children writing on topics of personal expertise and only later progresses to topics requiring research. The Reading and Writing Project recommends this sequence of units because, in our experience working with a huge range of student writers, we've observed that the process of research—reading about a topic, developing questions and looking for answers, synthesizing information, and paraphrasing what's been learned in one's own words—requires a complex set of skills, many of which are *only tangentially related to writing*. Most second graders first need the opportunity to grow their informational writing muscles—learning to organize information into categories and use a variety of elaboration strategies to teach—before undertaking the complexity of research. This way, we can first help them focus on lifting the quality of their nonfiction writing without having to teach research skills extensively.

There are, of course, many ways to journey through an initial informational writing unit of study in which children are writing about topics of personal expertise. One possible path might be as follows:

- ▶ Children are immersed in the *purpose, structure, features,* and *sound* of informational writing through reading aloud many nonfiction books and through writing informational texts together during shared writing.

- ▶ Children choose topics they know a lot about from their daily lives and imagine the audiences for their writing.

- ▶ Children rehearse, or plan, what they'll teach by making tables of contents.

- ▶ Children begin drafting chapters for a first informational book, learning strategies for saying more, or elaborating on information.

- ▶ Children begin drafting chapters for a second informational book, this time focusing on *making their teaching even clearer*, perhaps by carefully considering paper choice or by beginning to use paragraphs.

- ▶ Children select the book they like the best and revise it.

- ▶ Children edit their book for their readers, using editing checklists to check for punctuation, capitalization, and word wall words.

▶ Children "fancy up" their writing by adding color to their pictures, making a front cover, and perhaps making an About the Author page.

Using Read-Aloud to Promote Essential Understandings About Informational Texts

It makes sense to start our planning of any new unit of study in writing by studying existing examples of that genre. I strongly recommend to teachers that before beginning a unit of study on informational writing, they pore over nonfiction books asking two main questions: first, "What seems to be essential to teach in this genre?" and second, "What might I need to teach this particular group of writers that will help them make big strides toward proficiency in this genre?" The answer to the second question, of course, will be slightly different from year to year, and even unit to unit, based on the group of children and their prior experiences with informational writing. In studying the Common Core State Standards, and in working with my RWP colleagues and many teachers and in many classrooms far and wide, I gathered what feel to be some essentials in the teaching of informational writing.

1. Nonfiction writers write to teach their readers a lot of information as well as to make readers interested in their information.

2. Nonfiction writers use both text and additional features to teach information.

3. Nonfiction has a predictable structure of topic and subtopics.

4. Nonfiction texts have specific vocabulary that gives them an "expert" voice. The Common Core State Standards refer to this as "domain-specific" vocabulary.

As experienced nonfiction readers and writers, we can easily see these qualities inside of the nonfiction books we read. The goal of this work, then, is to get students to see these things, too. For instance, how might we get them to identify subtopics with ease? Or to identify an author's purpose for an index or text boxes? Or to begin to recognize and possibly internalize the vocabulary they need to develop a strong informational writing voice?

One way we can begin to support students in this work is with carefully planned, focused conversations and experiences we provide during read-aloud. The goal is to dig into texts in focused ways that help students to internalize some of the qualities of good informational writing.

Choosing mentor texts to read aloud and study closely

At the beginning of a unit, it is important to choose a few texts that will be read aloud and studied repeatedly throughout the study and that will serve as co-teachers, helping students imagine possibilities for their writing. It helps to make sure that the texts we choose look fairly similar to what our students will be trying to write themselves and that present a model that is within reach for our students. The following questions can be used as a guide to help choose appropriate mentor texts:

▶ Does the topic of at least one of my mentor texts show how a writer can teach about a topic of personal expertise? (e.g., *A Day at Gymnastics*, or *Baseball*)

▶ Does the book use an "I" teaching voice rather than an authoritative, third-person teaching voice?

▶ Is the text organized in a straightforward way, as in topics and subtopics?

▶ Is the syntax of the text simple enough that a child might listen to the text and think, "I could write a text like that"?

Think-alouds and turn-and-talks: opportunities to model and practice the strategies of proficient and thoughtful readers and writers

For a few days or so leading up to a writing unit of study, the teachers with whom I work carefully plan not only which books they will read during interactive read-aloud time but also *where* they will pause and think aloud. Many teachers mark these places with sticky notes. The think-aloud serves as a model to demonstrate what a proficient reader might think and do as she reads. It also provides an opportunity to model the ways that a writer attends to craft and structure as she reads. After reading a section of a nonfiction text, we might stop and think aloud about a writer's craft by saying something like, "Hmmm . . . I'm noticing that the writer here is talking to us as readers. Here, where she writes, 'Did you think that polar bears are snowy white?' it's almost like she's having a conversation with us!"

Just as it's important to provide modeling of the thinking of proficient readers through think-alouds, we'll want to provide opportunities for students to turn and talk with a partner on the rug, so that they have a chance to practice strategies we're teaching. If we've just done a think-aloud in which we paused to notice a writer's craft, we might then read on, pausing to give them time to talk with each other in ways that mirror the work we've just modeled. In this instance, after reading on we might prompt students, saying, "Wow, the author is still really trying to make us interested in this information, isn't she? Turn and tell your partner which places the author seems to be trying to make us interested in this information. What words is she using?" Listening in on partnerships as they turn and talk gives us invaluable insight into what they know, what they wonder, and what they need to learn.

Noticing and naming: time for students to attend to characteristics of informational texts

During read-aloud, we'll want to point out and discuss the functions of various features of nonfiction—tables of contents, headings, indexes, glossaries, and so on—especially if we haven't done this previously in the year. Second graders are often fascinated by the variety of layouts in nonfiction texts— eager to examine how one insect book is structured through question and answer, for example, while another is written like a diary.

With our support, students can also consider the rationale behind these features. We can help students consider purpose by asking questions like, "Why might the author have used bold letters for this word?" or, "How does this diagram help readers learn a lot about this topic?" Many teachers create a chart during read-aloud to which they can add throughout the unit to highlight the text features, their purposes, and examples.

Using Read–Aloud to Focus on the Structure and Language of Informational Texts

In the next two sections, we'll explore two other important read-aloud experiences that can support a wide range of students as informational writers before they even pick up a pencil. First, we'll plan read-aloud experiences that help students to discover and develop an understanding of a typical expository structure of topic and subtopics. Next, we will plan read-aloud experiences that explore and develop deeper understanding of the language typically used in nonfiction texts.

Read-aloud experiences that help students understand the structures of informational writing

When we, as proficient readers, pick up a book called *Planets Around the Sun*, we have definite expectations. First, we expect that the book will have subtopics, or various "chunks" of information. Second, we expect predictable kinds of subtopics—we will most likely be able to accurately predict what many of those subtopics will be (perhaps one chunk about the Sun, one chunk about the Earth, Mars, Venus, and so on). Even without a table of contents, which not all informational texts have, proficient readers will be able to find where one subtopic ends and the next begins.

What my colleagues and I have come to realize at the Reading and Writing Project is that many of our students, however, will *not* have such expectations. They will open a nonfiction book without anticipating such chunks of information and, even *with* a table of contents, may not notice or use these chunks of information to support their understanding of the text! Before students write informational texts, they need to understand that these texts are organized by topic and subtopics.

Because understanding and internalizing this structure is so critical to writing informational texts, students need plenty of opportunities to practice noticing and discussing structure in nonfiction books. This means that whenever I read a nonfiction book (starting in September), before opening the book and reading, I pause and think aloud, "How will this book go?" I could also word this question differently, saying, "What 'chunks' of information, or subtopics, do I anticipate?" My think-aloud for the book *Bees* in the second-grade class mentioned above sounded like this:

I held up the book and said, "Hmm . . . the title of this book is *Bees*. I wonder how this book will go? Maybe it will go like this: some pages teaching me about bee bodies, then some pages about what bees eat, then pages about where bees live. . . ."

If this book had a table of contents, I might then study that page with students, asking, "Was I right? Are some of these chapters the same as what I predicted?" Many books, like this one, don't have a table of contents, so after reading a page, I stopped to think aloud. "So, was I right? Is this page about bee bodies? I wonder what the next page will teach us about?"

After modeling this kind of thinking every time I read an informational book aloud, I soon ask students to try it with me, to predict the chapters or "parts" we think the book might contain. We might quickly jot our thoughts on a chart with our predictions and add new "parts" or chapters we discover the book actually has as we read. I then highlight for students the way these subtopics are organized logically—perhaps by thinking aloud about how the chapter titles seem to have the same structure or how these titles match the titles of other books on the same topic.

In developing this understanding of the structure of informational texts, repetition is key. It is not enough to spend one day modeling how a reader anticipates that a nonfiction book will have "parts" or "chapters." We must model and practice this kind of thinking from September on!

Read-aloud experiences that help students internalize the language of informational writing

Every genre has not only its own structure and conventions but also its own language, its own *sound*. We know that, as writers, we write with our ears. We write sentences and then reread them thinking, "Does that sound right?" We pay attention to rhythm and fluency as well as meaning. Reading aloud lots and lots of nonfiction texts can help our writers internalize the sound of nonfiction and develop an ear for informational writing.

Reading aloud to develop an "ear" for expository structure will go differently than reading to understand information. When I read aloud to gather information, I'll likely prompt students to turn and talk about what they're learning. I might say, "Hmm . . . let's take a few seconds to think about this. The author just gave lots of information about bee bodies. Turn and tell your partner what information you just learned about bee bodies from this section." These turn-and-talks are important to make meaning of the texts. However, if my goal is to call students' attention to the *sound* and *language* of informational text, I might plan a few different kinds of experiences.

First, we might study our nonfiction read-aloud book looking for phrases that are particular to nonfiction texts. Here we're looking less for content words (like *scales* or *antenna*) and more for general words found in many nonfiction texts that make the texts sound like nonfiction (like, *one example is* and *sometimes*). One analogy that I find useful when analyzing texts is to point out that some words are the "bricks" in a text while others are the "mortar" holding it together to make a structure. Kylene Beers points out that teaching students to attend to these "mortar" words can make a big difference in their reading comprehension and writing fluency

(Beers 2003). A search through *Bees!* turned up the following list:

> . . . is called . . .
> When . . .
> Also
> There are
> . . . can be used for . . .
> Some
> Sometimes
> Almost
> As many as
> About as many
> Other
> Up to

While some of these words are simply useful transitions, adverbs, and conjunctions that all nonfiction writers use, others can be used to signal specific nonfiction writing structures. When a writer is comparing things, for example, he or she might use words or phrases like: *on the other hand*, *similarly*, or *but*, whereas a writer who is teaching about a cause and its effects may use words such as *since*, *because*, and *this led to.* This unit is a good opportunity to expose second graders to these structures and transition words, even though most students will develop real fluency with these concepts down the road.

Of course, second graders won't internalize the language of nonfiction simply by making and reading lists of words! Children develop language and literary syntax by hearing it and using it in authentic contexts, through active engagement in learning and with repeated experiences.

The text *Navigating Nonfiction*, part of Lucy Calkins and Kathleen Tolan's *Units of Study for Teaching Reading, Grades 3–5* (2010), outlines one way to help writers engage actively and authentically with the language of expository writing. Teachers can pause in the midst of reading a text and ask children to envision and act out what they've just read. When I read aloud the book *Bees!* to the class of second graders, I stopped after reading this page:

> Leafcutter bees are big bees.
> They can be up to
> one and one-half inches long.
> But some bees are very small.
> You can hardly see them!

I wrote the words *up to*, *some*, and *hardly* on a chart. We discussed the meaning of each of these phrases and words briefly. "I'm going to read that again," I said. "Listen carefully to each sentence, trying to imagine what it's saying. Then you'll have a chance to act out the sentence with your partner."

After rereading the page, I asked students to turn and teach a partner what they'd learned. "Hold up your finger, like this! This is going to be your explaining finger. As you teach your partner, act out what you're teaching, so that your partner learns a lot."

I crouched next to Maria on the carpet as she turned to teach her partner. "I'm going to teach you about leafcutter bees," she began, holding her finger up to show she was going into her explaining and teaching mode. "They are big, but not that big, like one and a half inches long." She showed her partner with her fingers her approximation for one and a half inches. Then, she whipped up her finger again to teach her next point, "But some bees are so teeny tiny that you can't even see them except for with a microscope." Here, she made her hand into an improvised microscope and peered down into it.

The students and I became fully engrossed in that single page that day—reading, talking, and acting out with our hands and our partners. This helped them not only to understand the text better but also to incorporate these new phrases into their working vocabulary!

Shared Writing: A Time to Model and Practice Strategies for Writing Informational Texts

For some writers, reading a few examples of nonfiction will be enough for them to feel confident enough to dive in and begin writing their own. Others may benefit from watching their peers in action and by practicing thinking like a nonfiction writer. Shared writing can provide critical support for writers who need more scaffolds. These ten- to fifteen-minute writing sessions can happen either a few days prior to launching the informational text unit or in small groups once your unit has begun. Whether shared writing sessions happen during or outside of workshop time, it's critical to remember that shared writing does not replace or substitute for independent writing time. Instead, it takes place in addition to that time, and its purpose is to foreshadow and support the work your students will soon be doing independently.

In a shared writing session, the teacher alone holds the pen. This is in contrast to interactive writing, where the teacher shares the pen with student volunteers who take turns at writing the message (Fountas, McCarrier, and Pinnell 1999). In shared writing, the "shared" part involves composition, and the teacher and students think and talk together about what to write next and how to write it.

At P.S. 1, in Brooklyn, a second-grade teacher, Miss Liz, and I planned the following sequence of shared writing sessions as a way of preparing students for the challenge of getting started on an informational book:

Day 1: Choose a topic and begin a table of contents.

Day 2: Finish the table of contents and start writing one of the chapters.

Day 3: Finish one of the chapters.

For this shared writing experience, we chose a topic Miss Liz was confident that all of her students knew well from life experience—the school cafeteria! Shared writing goes smoothest when teachers choose topics that their students know well from their daily lives: All About School, All About the Playground, All About Winter, and so on.

Choose a topic and begin a table of contents

During each shared writing session, the teacher models the strategies she plans to introduce later in her minilessons and then has students try them together on the shared text. Throughout, she can provide important coaching for students.

Here's how I got Miss Liz's class kicked off on Day One of shared writing—composing a table of contents:

> I sat by a piece of chart paper that said "Table of Contents" on the top. "Okay, so we've decided that we're going to be teaching our parents in this book we're writing called *All About the Cafeteria*. One way writers start thinking about what they'll teach is they make a table of contents—a list of the parts, or chapters, that the book will teach about. One way writers think of possible chapters for their table of contents is by imagining their topic and then thinking, 'What do I really want people to know about this topic? What could I teach?' Let's see . . . our topic is 'All About the Cafeteria.' I want to picture what I could teach about this topic, so I'm going to make a kind of camera. (I make a "camera" with my hands over my eyes.) I'll imagine the cafeteria in my mind and look around with this pretend camera seeing what would make good parts for our book. Let's zoom in with our cameras and think, 'What do I see that I really want people to know? What can I teach?' I modeled looking around with my camera. "Hmm . . . what do I see? What can I teach? Oh! I see kids on the lunch line getting their food! So maybe one chapter can be 'The Lunch Lines.'"

In addition to choosing a topic the students know well, I made several other teaching moves, developed by the Reading and Writing Project, to make my demonstration especially clear. First, I explicitly *named a strategy* that students can use to generate chapters, or subtopics, for their topics. Then, I *used a gesture*—making a camera—to make the demonstration memorable and help ELLs activate language. I also used *repetition.* I asked the same questions over and over—What do I see? What can I teach?—to provide easy replication when I coach the students to try the strategies.

Next, I coached all the students to make a camera, cupping their hands together and closing their eyes to picture the topic—in this case, the cafeteria. I said, "Zoom your camera all around the cafeteria! Ask yourself, 'What do I see? What can I teach?'" Then, as students turned to a partner to talk about what they could teach, I crawled over to Lissette, a struggling writer, to coach her with this strategy.

M: What do you see? What could one of our chapters be?

L: (shrugs)

M: Close your eyes. Picture the cafeteria. Move your camera. . . . Now, stop! Do you see something? Do you see something you could teach?

L: The garbage cans. Throwing stuff away.

M: Great! (I point to the blank table of contents.) So one chapter could be . . .

L: "Garbage Cans."

M: Right! Or, "Throwing Away Lunch Trash." Now get your camera back up and look for something else!

Shared writing in second grade should be full of turn-and-talks. Allowing students to talk with a partner before sharing with the whole class gives the teacher an opportunity to provide coaching to individual students or partnerships that need more support with a strategy. Here, I not only coached Lissette step-by-step through the strategy, I also reinforced the strategy immediately by saying, "Now get your camera back up . . ." This repetition in our coaching enables students to develop more automaticity and independence with the strategies we teach.

At the end of the first day's shared writing, the table of contents looks like this:

All About the Cafeteria
Table of Contents
1. Lunch Lines
2. Throwing Away Lunch Trash
3. School Aides
4. Helping Friends at Lunch

The class certainly discussed many more possibilities for chapter titles than the final product shows. This is because shared writing focuses on the *thinking* work of writing—thinking what we could write, and then thinking of different ways we could write that. In other words, a class might spend ten minutes talking about different possibilities and in the end have only two sentences written down on the page! After hearing many students' ideas for possible chapter titles, I ultimately wrote down just three more ideas for titles, noting with a smile, "If I wrote down everyone's good ideas, I'd be writing all the way down to the floor!"

The time and care we take immersing our students in the structure and sound of nonfiction through read-aloud and shared writing will be critical to their ability to write informational texts. By carefully selecting mentor texts, planning focused read-aloud experiences, and providing modeling and practice through shared writing, we can be sure that we have provided a strong foundation for the wide variety of writers in our classes, putting them on a sure path to success in informational writing.

CHAPTER TWO

Getting Started

Choosing Topics, Planning a Draft, and Beginning to Write Chapters

After hearing so many fascinating nonfiction books read aloud and perhaps beginning to write a text with the class through shared writing, our students will be itching to write their own informational books. This chapter will help us get our unit off to a great start. I begin with a couple of important suggestions about the behind-the-scenes work we can do to get ready for the unit. Then, I'll offer ways to help our writers choose engaging topics and explain how to help them with the tricky work of planning a draft.

Gather and Create Materials Children Will Need to Write Informational Texts

There's a saying about how success materializes where preparation and opportunity meet. Nowhere is this more true than in the classroom! Though we will certainly use the unexpected "teachable moments" that arise daily in our classrooms, there's no substitute for preparation in being able to make these lessons stick long past that fleeting moment. It seems wise, then, to spend some time before the unit begins gathering what we'll need not only for the first few days of teaching but for the possibilities beyond, so that we're ready at just the right moment with the perfect paper for Isaiah to try a diagram that zooms in, or with the perfect example marked in a read-aloud to show Jasmine how nonfiction writers can use their five senses to teach more.

Supply writers with a variety of paper choices that support their writing

Making wise paper choices is something writers need to do all the time for any genre. For this reason, it's important to provide our students with the kind of paper that will channel them toward the sort of work we hope they will do. We'll want to consider providing paper that will support students in organizing their work as well as paper for publishing their pieces. For this unit, we'll want to look through our mentor texts to find the different kinds of page designs that are most typical of informational texts. We can use what we notice to create paper precisely tailored to our students' needs. Our paper supply for this unit may include:

- **Topic list paper.** This kind of paper serves as a scaffold for brainstorming possible writing topics. This paper could be a skinny half-sheet of paper, with lines that invite listing. Or we might encourage students to consider their audience as they generate topics by creating a two-column sheet with one side for possible topics and the other side for possible readers who might want or need to learn about such topics.

- **Table of contents paper.** Most second graders will have ideas for at least six possible chapters in their books, so we'll want to provide enough lines. (Many students will generate eight to ten chapter ideas, so be prepared for this as well!)

- **Chapter paper.** Some teachers find it helpful to make special paper for the start of a chapter, with a line for the chapter title or heading at the top, a space for a small picture, and then lots of lines on which the writer can teach what he or she knows about that subtopic. We'll want to have different paper choices available, each with a different number of lines.

- **A variety of paper layouts.** If students had exposure to many different types of layouts and paper choices in previous grades, then it may make sense to put out some of the paper choices from the preceding year. Possibilities may include diagram paper, four-box (or "kinds of") paper, and how-to paper.

Write our own informational text to use for demonstration

Prior to the start of the unit, it's helpful to write our own informational book, one that can be used as a demonstration text during minilessons and conferences. Although we'll demonstrate generating ideas for topics, making a table of contents, drafting chapters, and thinking aloud in front of our students, this does not mean we simply "make it up" in front of our students! One suggestion we give at the Reading and Writing Project is for teachers to work through the writing process together in their grade meetings as part of planning for the unit. Teachers often turn part of their meeting time into a writing workshop and then use parts of what they've written as demonstration text in their classrooms. As part of their teaching, teachers can retrace the steps they went through to make the draft within a sequence of minilessons.

In one school, teachers sat together in a grade meeting with the paper choices they intended to give their own students. They began with topic choice, thinking, "What do *I* know a lot about? What could *I* teach?" They considered how they might teach about knitting, or grandchildren, or yoga. Each teacher selected a topic, and after a few moments, the room was filled with the sound of pens scratching. After writing for a bit, they talked about some of the strategies they used to elaborate and what seemed hard about writing nonfiction. As one teacher reflected, "Going through the writing process myself makes it more real when I say in my minilessons, 'This is what I do when I write . . .' And I really mean it when I say to my struggling students, 'I know! Writing *can* be hard!'"

Writers Choose Topics by Considering Areas of Expertise, Audience, and Focus

Many second graders have no trouble generating ideas for potential informational books. They are knowledgeable and passionate about any number of topics and will be quick to say, "I'll teach about baseball!" or "I'll write about dinosaurs!" Some students, on the other hand, may struggle to uncover topics in which they are truly invested. This next section provides a few ideas for those who need extra help.

Writers think, "What do I know a lot about? What could I teach other people?"

We want, first and foremost, for each writer to choose a topic that is meaningful to him or her. If our young writers begin this unit without a clear passion for their topics, we can be sure that the writing will be, at the very least, lackluster and monotonous, and, at the very worst, an uphill struggle to get anything down on the page at all.

One way students can generate ideas for topics is by asking themselves questions such as, "What do I love? What do I know a lot about that I could teach others?" If a student goes to karate every Saturday, then that's something he knows about—a possible topic. If a student has a new baby brother, then that becomes a perfect topic choice for that student. We want our classrooms to reflect our students' lives and for our libraries to be filled with student-authored books about topics that are meaningful to them: having a pet, reading chapter books, playing drums, preparing Mexican food, riding scooters.

Some writers will list very general topics, such as school, dogs, and families. To help these writers find more specific areas of expertise, staff developers at the Reading and Writing Project often suggest having writers carry tiny notepads for a few days (much like the ones they might have carried during the Authors as Mentors unit) and record things they know a lot about. We can tell them, "Writers are *always* on the look-out for good topics! I'm going to give you these tiny notepads to record things you know a lot about. You might think of topics at recess, home, the grocery store—anywhere!" We can model how to jot topics in a notepad, perhaps taking a walking trip with the class around the school, or going out for a few moments at lunch and having students stop and jot (or sketch) the things they see and do that they know all about.

Writers consider their audience by thinking, "Who will my reader be?"

Youngsters can imagine possible writing topics by thinking about the topics that might interest their audience. They can ask, "What would my readers want to know more about?" When I approached Angelica in a conference on the first day of the unit, her list had one topic on it, All About Second Grade, which was the topic of her class' shared writing text. I pulled a chair close and began my conference:

M: Angelica, you sure know about second grade! Who would you write that book for? Who do you think would need to learn all about second grade?

A: (Thinks for a moment.) My baby sister don't go to this school.

M: Wow. So you are thinking that you could write her a book that would teach her what second grade is like because she doesn't come here? What a smart idea! Writers think of who might read their books and what they might teach their readers. Is there something else that you think you could teach your baby sister all about? What else do you know about that she needs to know?

A: (Looks down at her fingers.) She don't never put paint on her fingers or makeup, and I could teach her about that.

M: Oh, really? You think you could write a book called "All About Makeup?" Add it to your list, and keep thinking of what else you could teach your sister all about.

When Angelica generates topics for a specific reader or group of readers she knows well, chances are good that she'll generate more topics she knows well or topics on which she'll be able to elaborate more fully.

Writers can focus by choosing one part of a topic, or one idea they have about that topic

Many proficient writers come to us in second grade after having written "All About Dogs" or "All About Soccer" in first grade (and maybe even in kindergarten, too). To ratchet up topic choice for these writers, we can show them that writers don't have to write "all about" a topic, but instead they may think first about what's *really* important for their readers to know, then choose one *part* of that topic or one *idea* they have about that topic and write all about that part or idea.

In one small group on the first day of the unit, I gathered together four writers and showed them the ways various professional writers had focused their books about sharks. One had chosen to write about just one kind of shark, while another had written about just one idea about sharks:

> Writers, I was looking through our classroom library yesterday when I realized that we have a lot of books about sharks, but they're each a little bit different. This book is called *Sharks!*, while this one is called *Great White Sharks*. This one is called *Shark Attacks*, while this one is called *A Shark Pup Grows Up*. And when I was looking through the alphabet book basket, I found this one: *Sharkabet: A Sea of Sharks from A to Z!* It started me thinking about how writers can write to teach not just all about something, but they can teach about one part, or one kind of that topic. Or they can teach about one idea they have about that topic.

Then, I asked them to turn to a partner and think whether there was a part of their topic they could focus on or one idea that was important for their readers to know about their topics. One student, Rolando, realized he could just focus on fairy-tale books instead of writing "All About Reading," while Gina realized that instead of "All About Dogs," she could make a whole book about the smart and cool tricks that dogs do.

We can help our writers focus their topics in this way in small groups before they generate a list of topics, after they've made this list, or even after they've written a few tables of contents. Of course, we may notice that some writers will do this kind of focusing work automatically, even without our teaching!

Once the students have spent a day or two generating ideas for topics, we can help them to zoom in on a topic. We might say, "Writers, tomorrow we're going to start making a plan for how our books will go. You've come up with many ideas for what you might write about. Take a look at some of those ideas and think, 'Which topic do I feel most expert in? Which topic do I know *a lot* about that I could teach others? Which of these topics really *matters* to me?'" While children discuss their choices with a partner, we might make a quick list of students who will need even more one-on-one support the next day to land on a strong topic.

Writers Organize Their Information: Generating Subtopics and Making Tables of Contents

A key part of writing informational texts is organizing the information into categories. The Common Core State Standards suggest that second graders write informational texts in which they develop a topic with points—in other words, that they expand on a topic by putting information into categories. Often it is helpful for writers to plan these categories before they begin to draft. Some teachers use tools to help students organize subtopics before they start writing—showing students how to use webs, lists, and other graphic organizers. It's important to point out, however, that these graphic organizers are simply tools. Giving a blank web to a student who intends to write about math and suggesting he writes "Math" in the middle does not solve the inevitable problem of what exactly goes in the bubbles around the middle! This means we need to support students in not only how to use the tools but also the kind of thinking that is necessary to use those tools effectively.

Strategies to help writers develop tables of contents

Some of the most valuable work this unit holds is the process students learn through making tables of contents. Tables of contents, by their structure, require students to think about a topic's important components. We can have our writers flex their brains over and over in this way by asking them to generate a few possible tables of contents. This also ensures that they choose a topic about which they have sufficient interest and expertise. In this section, I'll present a few strategies that my colleagues and I have found successful to help second-grade students generate subtopics—or what I'll call here "chapter titles"—for a table of contents. I recommend showing students a few strategies in one day, helping them understand that any one of these strategies can help them accomplish the job of planning what information they'll teach.

Writers think of chapter titles by thinking, "What do I know about my topic?"

A writer working on a table of contents about "Soccer" could use this strategy to think of a few different chapter titles, saying, "I know how to make a goal, and I know the jobs that the players have. I know the kinds of snacks you get at halftime."

Writers think of chapter titles by picturing their topic in their mind and then thinking, "What do I see? What can I teach?"

This is the strategy I modeled during the shared writing in Chapter 1. Writers picture their topics, move their "camera" around and say, "What are the parts of my topic? What do I see that I want others to know about my topic? What could I teach?" A writer picturing "Soccer," for example, might "see": soccer balls, coaches, players, cleats, uniforms.

Writers think of chapter titles by thinking, "What do I do with my topic?" or "What does my topic do?"

This strategy might seem strange at first until writers have had several chances to practice it. A student thinking of what they do in "Soccer" may think of: practices, playing games, getting dressed, scoring a goal, passing, dribbling. A second grader thinking, "What does my cat do?" came up with these chapter titles: "Cats Eat," "Cats Play," "Cats Have Kittens." (See Figure 2.1 for another student's example of this strategy.)

It's important to mention here that for some ELLs or struggling writers in our classes, making a table of contents before writing about a topic might not be appropriate. For these students, creating a separate table of contents page may be too abstract. They might struggle to connect the process of making a table of contents to its purpose, which is to plan what they will teach their readers. These writers might be better able to plan their writing if we give them a stapled, three-page booklet with paper much like the Small Moments paper (with a box at the top for a picture and lines

I'm writing a all about __ice skating__

Table of Contents

- very tight shoes! 1
- special shoes! 2
- march, march and away! 3
- push, push and glide! 4
- stop! 5
- turns and turning! 6
- glossary 7
- index 8
- spinning time! 9

FIG. 2.1 *Kobena's Table of Contents*

on the bottom for words). We can have these writers sketch or write one word at the top of each page of the booklet to tell three things they want to teach their readers. The students can then either make another booklet to plan how another topic might go, or they can get started working on that first booklet as their first informational book.

Writers Get Started on a Draft

Once writers have made a plan for how their information will be organized by creating a table of contents, they are ready to start drafting. (It's important to note that these tables of contents may, and probably will, be revised as we draft—writers always leave room for revision!)

There are lots of ways to get drafts started. We can have students reread their tables of contents to decide which chapter they'll write first (since they don't have to write their chapters in order!). One teacher got her students started with the same strategy they had practiced over and over during shared writing. Other teachers might try a new strategy. Here are two possibilities:

Writers picture the chapter title in their mind, and think, "What do I see? What could I teach about that?"

In this minilesson, you might pull the students close and begin:

> Writers, we've spent this week really thinking, "What are the things we know about from our lives that we can teach other people?" And yesterday, you chose one of your topics to try to start teaching about first. When I took them home last night, I got so excited thinking about the basket of new books we're going to have in our library—books that teach us all about scooters, and fairy tales, and Bratz dolls, and basketball games! Today, I want to teach you that writers get started on their drafts by choosing one of the

chapters they want to teach about and writing the chapter title at the top of their paper. Then they close their eyes and picture their chapter title. They zoom in close with their camera and they think, "What do I see? What can I teach about that?"

I want you to watch how I picture my chapter title in my mind, zoom in close, and think, "What do I see? What can I teach about that?"

After modeling it in our own book, *All About Tea* or *Running Road Races*, for instance, students can try the strategy with us on the class book *About Second Grade*.

Writers add lots of specific details to their pictures, then they teach about what they added in their words

I modeled this strategy in one classroom at P.S. 178 in Manhattan, holding a fat marker in my hand while I examined my sketch, thinking aloud:

Hmm . . . what else do I know about running shoes? Well, the bottom is a little bit thick, and it's kind of bumpy on the bottom, so let me add that. What else? Oh, and mine have a design on the side and some words that say "New Balance." Okay, I added lots of details to my picture, so now I can teach about those details in my words!

I said the words aloud as I wrote:

Running shoes have a thick bottom that is soft. They also have bumps on the bottom to grip onto mud so you don't slip. Some running shoes are made by a company called New Balance, and some are made by other companies.

By the time we send our students off to try either of the strategies above in their own books, they're off to a great start on their drafts.

It might be tempting to discount the importance of these first days in the unit. We may feel like having students make lists of topics and writing tables of contents isn't *really* writing, like we need to quickly get through this stuff to get started on the *real* writing in this unit. But this couldn't be further from the truth. Learning to see our lives in such a way that we are able to find the tiniest slices as precious possible topics for writing is some of the most important and fundamental work writers do. Helping second graders discover and strengthen new writing "muscles" for organizing information and generating subtopics lays the foundation upon which all future informational writing work will rest. We are establishing habits and skills upon which students will build for the rest of their writing lives.

CHAPTER THREE

Saying More

Elaboration in Informational Writing

Over the next week or two, we will focus primarily on helping our students to become better "teachers" with their writing. We'll want them to learn to elaborate: to say more and write more. However, we need to be careful what we wish for and, more important, what we teach toward! That is, if we teach second graders to write more simply for the sake of writing more about their topics, we will surely see writing that is repetitive and muddled.

Instead we must be zealous in our focus on the author's purpose when we teach elaboration. We'll strive to be sure our nonfiction writers are asking themselves the important, audience-driven questions: "What might my reader love to know more about? How can I make my writing clearer and more interesting?" instead of encouraging writers to merely think, "How can I try today's teaching point?" or, "Where can I add more words?"

Assembling a Toolbox of Elaboration Strategies

Over the next two weeks, our writers will need two different kinds of elaboration strategies:

- ▶ Strategies that help writers to say even more about their topic, or in other words, that increase the *amount* of information they give
- ▶ Strategies that help writers incorporate different informational text structures and features, or in other words, that increase the *variety* of information they give

Though I group the strategies together here according to these two purposes, we need not organize our teaching in this particular order. We'll want to organize our teaching based on our students and their needs. Many workshop teachers create charts such as the one on page 57 to record each strategy as it's been taught, finding that such a list encourages students to draw not only on today's minilesson but also on the repertoire of strategies they have been introduced to throughout the unit.

Strategies nonfiction writers use to teach more in each chapter

The following strategies are designed to help writers be purposeful as they add more to their writing. Although designed for informational writing, many of the strategies can be generalized and applied to any kind of writing that needs elaboration.

Writers give minilectures about their topics to themselves or to a partner

Many teachers who have worked with the Reading and Writing Project have found that rehearsing for writing by saying aloud what they will write helps young writers to "prime" their writing pump. This process is described explicitly in *Small Moments: Personal Narrative Writing* by Lucy Calkins and Abby Oxenhorn (2003). In narrative units, we often use partner planning time to have children storytell to their partners. Additionally, in informational writing units, as described in *Nonfiction Writing: Procedures and Reports* by Lucy Calkins and Laurie Pessah (2003), we can use partner planning time for students to *teach* their topic to their partner, helping them to elaborate as much as possible before going off to write.

We'll want to give our writers scaffolds to support them in giving these oral "minilectures." In one classroom, after the day's minilesson, I leaned forward and said, "Writers, can you take out your tables of contents for a minute? Sometimes it helps me before I write something to say aloud what I know about my topic and what I think I'll write. Right now I want you to touch the title of the chapter that you're going to be writing today. Think about what you know about that that you can teach someone. Maybe you'll use some of the nonfiction words that we wrote up on this chart, like, *Sometimes . . .* or *One example is . . .* Okay, now turn and talk to your partner. Try to teach them as much you can about that chapter."

Writers gather artifacts to help them remember what they know about their topic and practice teaching it to others

We can also help our students elaborate even more in these minilectures by asking them to bring in objects and pictures that go with their topics—basketballs, hockey sticks, dog leashes, trophies and so on. Students can hold these and teach their partners about their pictures and objects. During these lectures, we might be listening in and coaching, saying, "Point to something else on those swimming goggles you've brought. Teach me about that part," or, "Writers also teach why something is important. Can you teach your partner a little bit about why your dog leash is important?"

Writers can teach even more by rereading what they wrote and thinking to themselves, "What else could I teach about that?"

When it comes to informational writing, second-grade writers can be the ultimate minimalists. In a chapter on "Quarterbacks," Reign, who spends a great deal of time playing football with his friends, first wrote about the nicknames for quarterbacks, then wrote simply, "Sometimes the QB tricks people by running the ball." Reign, like many of our writers, can profit greatly from consistent, gentle coaching to stay even longer on one idea.

On this day, Reign's teacher pulled close to him, saying, "Reign, you know so much about football and what

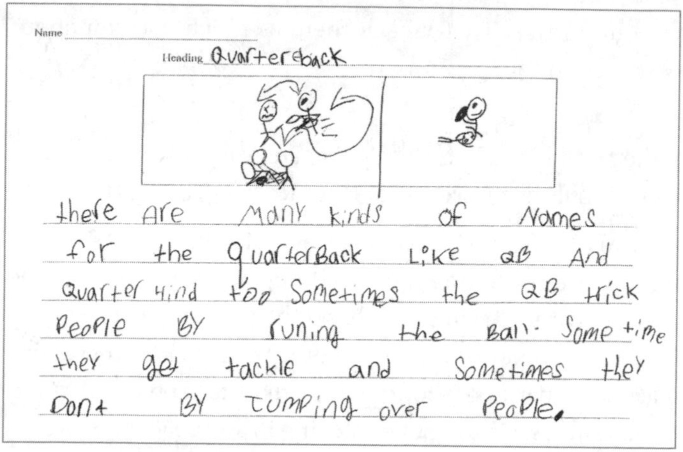
Name

Heading Quarterback

there are many kinds of Names
for the quarterBack Like QB And
Quarter hind too Sometimes the QB trick
People BY runing the Ball. Some time
they get tackle and Sometimes they
Dont BY Tumping over People.

FIG. 3.1 *Reign's Elaboration*

quarterbacks do! Can you reread each fact, then let's stop and think, 'What else could I teach about that?' to say even more?" This is the part of the coaching where we encourage writers to flex the "muscles" we developed earlier in the unit, and where some of those "mortar" nonfiction words that Kylene Beers talks about can be helpful. After his teacher provided him with some sentence starters, like, *Sometimes* . . . or *When* . . . , Reign found he could say a whole lot more about running a quarterback sneak. (See Figure 3.1.)

Writers make their facts specific

This strategy was first described by Lucy Calkins and Laurie Pessah in *Nonfiction Writing: Procedures and Reports*. As readers, we can predict that nonfiction writing will contain certain kinds of specific, predictable information—such as names, numbers, and sizes. In one minilesson, after pointing out many examples of these kinds of specific details in a read-aloud text, the teacher held up her chapter called "Feeding Dogs." "Let me look at my facts," the teacher thought aloud, "It says here 'Dogs eat dog food.' That doesn't sound very specific! Can I teach even more by thinking of names? Hmm . . . what are *names* of different dog food? Or maybe I can teach the *names* of the things I use to feed my dog."

Of course, when teaching this as a minilesson, we'll want to offer a broad array of ways to make facts more specific beyond just names! We'll coach writers to think, "Are there numbers that go with this fact?" as well as how to use their senses to teach more by thinking, "What does this topic look like, sound like, or feel like?"

In his book, *Drums Are Cool*, Jonah worked hard to teach his readers specific details about each drum, describing specifically how each one looks and sounds (see Figure 3.2), while Max's page describing Jack Russell terriers describes with precision a terrier's ears, coloring, and tails (see Figure 3.3).

Writers use stories to help them teach more about their topics

My colleagues and I at the Reading and Writing Project have recently begun inviting young nonfiction writers to make their information more clear and engaging for their readers by asking them to use those same story-writing muscles they worked so hard to strengthen at the beginning of the year in units of study such as Small Moments or Personal Narrative.

2. Tom Toms

The tom tom is like bongs only one thing you hit it with stiks and not hands. it makes a sound that souds lik a spoon Banging on a pot.

FIG. 3.2 *Jonah uses specific facts to elaborate.*

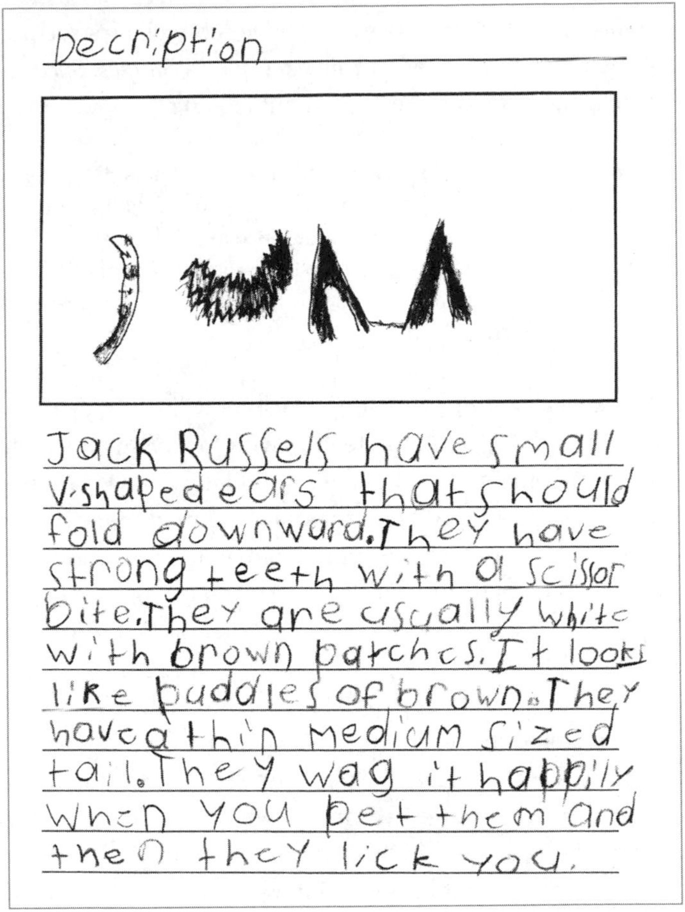

Decription

Jack Russels have small
V-shaped ears that should
fold downward. They have
strong teeth with a scissor
bite. They are usually white
with brown patches. It looks
like puddles of brown. They
have a thin medium sized
tail. They wag it happily
when you pet them and
then they lick you.

FIG. 3.3 *Max elaborates with specific facts.*

Nonfiction writers often use a narrative, storytelling structure to teach information, as in this example in *Sniffles, Sneezes, Hiccups, and Coughs* by Penny Durant (2005):

> When you sneeze, you take a deep breath. (That is the "ah" part.) You hold your breath as your chest muscles tighten. The pressure of the air in your lungs increases. You close your eyes. Your tongue presses against the roof of your mouth. Suddenly your breath comes out fast through your nose. (That is the "choo" part.)

Experienced writing workshop teachers will recognize this instantly as bit-by-bit storytelling, with lots of small action and even some story language ("Suddenly . . ."). When I pulled one group of writers together and read them Penny Durant's chapter about sneezing, I turned to them and said, "Writers, when I first read this part, I could just picture in my mind that sneeze! I could see the first little thing that happens . . ." I took a deep breath to illustrate. "And then the next little thing that happens," I gasped and held my breath. "And I pictured the next thing and the next. Couldn't you just picture it, too? That really helped me to remember the information I was learning! I wonder if we could do this in our own nonfiction writing? Do you think you could find a part in your book that might be a little bit like a movie and then tell what happens bit by bit so that your readers can really picture it in their minds?"

Alexis, a struggling writer, quickly became engrossed in storytelling the way a bombardier beetle poisons and then eats its prey, and added the small moment to his book. (See Figure 3.4.)

> The bombardier is important because his habitat is dangers it has chemicals and it puts chemicals in it's habitat and if a bug steps on it the bug gets poison and it kills the bug who steps on it. the Bombardier idoes. that to poison a bug and eats it the bombardien habitat is so dangers that not even one bug has come out.

FIG. 3.4 *Alexis uses storytelling to elaborate his chapter about bombadier beetles.*

Writers always think about their audiences and how they want the audience to feel and think about the information

Informational writing at its best is far more than a catalogue of facts. Often, even informational writers have an "angle," or an agenda. The first page of Jennifer Dussling's *Bugs! Bugs! Bugs!* (2011) from DK Readers begins:

> Yikes! Most bugs look scary close up. But *you* don't need to worry. Most bugs are a danger only to each other. They are the bugs that really bug other bugs.

This writer has a clear angle. She wants us to stop being afraid of bugs. She wants us to understand how bugs are truly dangerous only to each other.

We can teach our students to reread each page of their books carefully, thinking, "How do I want my readers to feel about this information? What do I want them to think?"

Maybe a writer who is writing about taking care of a baby sister wants her readers to think that sometimes baby sisters can be annoying. She can reread her chapter on "Changing Diapers" and add responses to her facts, so that her original text, which read:

> Sometimes when you have a baby sister you have to change her diaper. It is smelly. You have to use wipes and put on a new one.

now sounds like this:

> Sometimes when you have a baby sister you have to change her diaper. Eeew! It is smelly. You have to use wipes and put on a new one. You probably won't like it.

She can even revise her chapter title to incorporate this idea—"Changing Diapers Is Annoying"—to affect her readers even more. Writers can change their readers' minds by adding personal responses, exclamations, and even questions, as a second grader named Claire did:

> Recycling is important to take care of the earth. What do you think the world would be like if everyone just left their trash around? Yuck!

Writers who truly care about their topics are passionate about affecting their readers' hearts and minds. They use their facts to expand their readers' thinking, and even to rally them to action!

Earlier this year, I visited a second-grade class in Brooklyn and pulled a chair close to Tenesi, watching her pencil fly across the page. When there was a slight pause in her torrent, I leaned forward.

"I've got to know," I said, "What are you teaching about?"

"I'm teaching about brothers," Tenesi said, pointing to the two taller boy figures flanking the single girl figure in the picture.

"Have you thought at all about who you might be making this book for? Who's going to need to read it to learn?" I asked.

"It's for my aunt," Tenesi explained. "She only has girls." As we talked about what she was planning to write next, Tenesi suddenly jumped up and grinned. "I know!" she said. "I'm going to write, 'Brothers sometimes are dirty. And you need to tell them to wash their hands,' because then when she watches us she'll know, and they won't dirty up her sofa anymore!"

With an engaging topic, a clear sense of her audience, and a growing toolkit of elaboration strategies, Tenesi is well on her way to becoming the kind of nonfiction writer we're all trying to grow—one clearly focused on providing her reader with important information, a writer who clearly believes in the power of her teaching to change the world.

Structures nonfiction writers use to teach more about their topics

So far, the strategies I've listed have focused primarily on the important work of encouraging our students to say more inside of each of their chapters. However, this unit also offers us the opportunity to teach students that nonfiction writers have a variety of structures and page layouts available to them and that these are important tools in each writer's repertoire. The trick here lies in introducing students to these structures while avoiding the unwanted effect of a class set of identical informational books, with every writer's book structured in exactly the same way. Much of the magical pull that nonfiction books have on young readers lies in their utter uniqueness, so it makes sense that we'd want our students' books to be just as unique from *each other*.

My colleague at the RWP, Jen Serravallo, developed a useful system for keeping her students from falling into a rut of "cookie-cutter" informational books. For a week during her writing workshop, Jen invited children to select topics they wanted to study in seminars, offering her minilessons to small groups of interested students who asked to study that particular topic. To help students to choose a topic to study, she showed examples of the kinds of structures that would be covered in each seminar and asked students to think carefully about which structures might best fit their topics. Students could chose between Monday's seminar on How-Tos, or Tuesday's seminar on Before/After diagrams, and so on. To avoid a popularity effect where students all signed up for the same few seminars, Jen limited the spots available on each sign-up sheet, and she strongly encouraged more struggling students to sign up for the seminars that would most closely match their writing strengths and needs.

Whether we teach the following lessons as whole-group minilessons or small-group seminars, we'll want to convey to our students that nonfiction writers make very specific choices about pages and structures to include in their books. By the end of the unit, second-grade writers can and should be able to tailor the structure of their writing to their topics and the audience for whom it's designed.

Writers use a variety of paper layouts and structures to make their teaching even more interesting and clear

Whether or not we use small-group seminars, we should spend some time studying our nonfiction mentor texts with an eye toward teaching writers to craft more engaging or clearer versions of these nonfiction features. In schools where writing workshops thrive across the grades, many of our writers have already used how-to, diagram, or "four-box" paper in previous grades, and we can support their use of familiar paper structures by teaching them to lift the level of work they do using these paper choices. Here are a few ideas for ways to "ratchet up" two of the typical pages second graders may want to include in their books:

▶ **How-to page.** Though children may have had experience with procedural writing, or how-tos, in previous grades, some of them will in all likelihood still need our help learning to visualize and write each step with ample precision. One way to ratchet up our writers' approach to this structure might also be to study mentor texts to learn how published authors use precise vocabulary and definitions to explain well.

▶ **Text features.** A key type of elaboration, and one that the Common Core State Standards highlight in depth, is adding text features that teach more about the topic. Chances are that our writers have been making diagrams, with a big picture in the middle and labels sticking out the sides, since kindergarten. We can stretch second-grade writers' thinking about what a diagram can be by studying mentor texts. In one classroom, I used Penny Durant's *Sniffles, Sneezes, Hiccups, and Coughs* (2005). I pulled children close to look at a diagram of the respiratory system. Children noticed how the illustrator shows both the outside and inside of the boy's face and chest by using light colors for his outsides and darker colors and lines for his insides. Then I pointed to the text box next to the word *diaphragm*. I said, "This diagram teaches a lot more than just the name of something. This text box gives information about the parts of the picture and really helps readers learn even more. Do you think you could make a diagram that teaches facts about the parts of your picture?" We can teach writers to add text boxes to support their diagrams, again drawing on mentor texts for support. Or, we may want to focus a bit on the ways in which mentor authors use "pictures that teach" in their how-tos. Writers often use zoomed-in pictures, with arrows to make their teaching even more clear.

Writers use data—and they get new ideas by collecting even more

In this unit, our writers are "experts" in their topics, writing without needing to do much research. Imagine the flood of new ideas that could ensue, however, if our nonfiction writers began to collect just a little bit of data about their topics and used it to elaborate on or focus their writing. In a classroom in Queens, a teacher had one small group of students devise surveys to gather more information about their topics. The room was abuzz as writers developed survey questions such as "Do you root for the Yankees or the Mets?" "Do you have a short-haired or long-haired cat?" "Do you like cleaning your room?"

As students fanned out over the classroom and the school with their surveys, they began to see their topics through new eyes. When they returned to the classroom the teacher asked the students to talk about the information they'd gathered and whether it had changed their thinking about what their books should include. One writer announced, "I learned that most boys think gymnastics is dumb. But there are lots of boys who do gymnastics in the Olympics! I'm going to make a chapter about 'Boy Gymnasts.'" Another said, "Most kids eat Chinese and Mexican food, but not very many said they eat Thai food. I'm going to add more about that to my book."

Writers can use the data they've collected as stand-alone chapters in their books, with one page being the results of a survey or graph, or they can weave the data they've gathered into their other chapters. This particular group of writers enjoyed collecting data so much that they continued their reader-driven stance by surveying their peers, "What questions do you have about my topic?" and then writing an FAQ, or frequently asked questions, page. (See Figure 3.5.)

Writers talk to other experts about their topic and ask, "What else can I teach about my topic?"

When asked for advice on writing nonfiction, Russell Freedman recommends that you "soak yourself in your research until it is seeping out of your pores" (Robb 2004). Though our writers may be experts in their topics already, we can help

> **Facts about the Arctic**
>
> Why is the Arctic mostly dark?
> because the Sun Shines at the oposite direction
> of the earth.
> Do people live in the Arctic?
> No because only sicentist come to
> study the Arctic but they dont live
> in the Arctic.
> IS their Plant eaters in the ArctIC?
> NO.
> Do reptile in the ArctIC?
> No.
>
> Web Sites WWW. Google.com then go to Artic
> after that go to images and
> you could See Arctic animals.

FIG. 3.5 *Example of One Writer's FAQ Page*

them "soak" themselves in their topics even more by suggesting they interview another "expert" on their topic.

Children can interview people in their lives who have
experience with their topics. A child writing about baseball
can plan to interview his Little League coach about how
coaches organize tryouts or about the play-calling signs they
use during games. A child writing about cats can interview
her mom about what she remembers about the shelter their

cat came from or the kinds of cat food she sees at the grocery store.

If we choose to have students interview others, it's helpful to remember that second graders are likely to be new at this. We can give them lots of practice by providing opportunities for the class to interview each other, school staff, or visitors. To get them started, we should help them learn to develop three or four good questions, speak clearly, ask people to please repeat their answers slowly, or ask follow-up questions, such as "Can you say more about that?" The information gathered from the interview can be published directly as an interview page in the book, *A Conversation with Coach Smith*, or the information can be woven throughout the book, with more proficient writers perhaps learning how to quote a source in their informational text.

Any one of the above teaching points can be extended over more than one day. Teaching second graders to try a strategy once is usually not too tricky. Teaching them to do it well, in the right place, for the right purpose, requires a bit more. Successful teachers I work with teach a strategy, then watch the students closely to see how they're trying the strategy and what possible finer points they might be missing. The teachers then plan to reteach the strategy the following day, angling their teaching toward that finer point.

CHAPTER FOUR

Preparing to Publish
Revision, Conventions, and Editing in Informational Writing

S econd graders are at an exciting time of growth in their writing. They're writing with more fluency and confidence than ever before. This newfound fluency not only enables them to sustain and develop their writing about a topic but also frees them up to consider the possibilities of revision. It's not uncommon to find writing in second-grade classrooms that looks like an exploding spiderweb, with "revision strips" taped every which way, as writers are both eager and able to reconsider the content and structure of their writing with greater ease. (See Figure 4.1.)

In this chapter I'll offer some ideas on teaching our students to revise their informational writing—including how to teach critical features such as introductions, conclusions, and developing titles. I'll also offer some ideas for teaching con-

FIG. 4.1 *Jaden tapes in revision strips.*

ventions that lend themselves particularly well to the informational writing unit. And last, I'll offer tips that support students as they apply those conventions we've taught them throughout the unit while editing their writing.

Revision in Informational Writing

One way we might kick off revision in this unit is to teach our students that writers choose their *best* pages to revise and publish—often around five or six pages. We can, of course, choose to have our students publish all of the pages they've written, but the winnowing process ensures that each page has the opportunity to receive the careful revision it deserves.

Teachers generally spend between two and three days revising before going on to edit and publish student writing. We might consider pursuing a couple of goals during these few days. First, we'll want our writers to read and reread their writing with two questions in mind: "Is my writing clear enough for my reader to understand?" and "Can I somehow make this more interesting for my reader?"

Revision can also be a time to begin writing (and/or revising) those parts of books that authors generally save for last—dedication pages, titles, tables of contents, and, in the case of many nonfiction books, introductions and conclusions. With these goals in mind, here are a few teaching points to consider as writers begin to make their way toward publishing.

Writers revise by thinking, "What are all the strategies I know to make my writing clear and interesting?"

Often, our revision process does not start with introducing brand-new strategies. Rather, we as teachers help our writers remember that they already have *lots* of strategies available to revise their writing. One option might be to have our students reread the strategy charts we've made throughout the unit. This can help them think about how they might do even *more* of what they've already learned to do as writers. Then the writers can get together with their partners and plan ways to make each page of writing teach more through thoughtful revision. Teachers can use this exercise as an opportunity to coach writing partnerships, encouraging each writer to make suggestions to his or her partner of other potential strategies the writer might try.

At this point in the unit, our chart might look something like this:

Squeeze Your Brain!!
Ways to Teach a Lot in Your Chapters:

▶ Picture your topic in your mind, make a camera, and zoom in on one thing. Think, "What could I teach someone about that?"

▶ Add to your picture, then think, "What could I teach about that?"

▶ Reread the heading and think, "What else could I teach someone about that?"

▶ Use your senses! Think, "What does it look like?"
"What does it sound like?"
"What does it feel like?"

▶ Make your pictures teach a lot!
Use labels!
Zoom in!
Use arrows!

▶ Make a comparison to help your reader understand even more.

▶ Think of numbers, names, and shapes that go with your topic.

▶ Reread and think, "How do I want my readers to feel about this information? What do I want them to think?"

▶ Use some nonfiction language, like Gail Gibbons!
• "Some pumpkins are . . ."
• "Most pumpkins are . . ."
• "One example is . . ."

After having partners plan the strategies they'll use, send students off to revise their chapters. Be sure to have on hand lots of tape and "revision strips"—strips of paper students can tape to their draft (lined for revising text, blank for revising pictures)—to be prepared for the blitz of revision that will ensue.

Once writers have reread and reconsidered their writing for a day or two, they're ready to consider how they might add more structural components such as introductions, conclusions, and titles.

Writers sometimes write an introduction to their book by telling their reader what they will learn and why it might be important to know this

An introduction acts as a roadmap for readers for their journey ahead, telling them what they'll learn as they read. It can also set up the reader for the important work of changing readers' hearts and minds about a topic.

Lissette's book starts with an introduction that not only tells her readers what they'll learn but also persuades her readers to care very deeply about the topic at hand. (See Figure 4.2.)

For her book, *Birthday Parties,* Stephanie considered carefully not only what her readers would learn but also who might be interested in this information. She wrote:

> Are you a kid who never gets invited to birthday parties?
> Do you wish you were going to a party every day?
> This book will tell you everything you need to know.
> Let's party!

It's important to read several introductions together with students so that they can really get a sense of the voice and

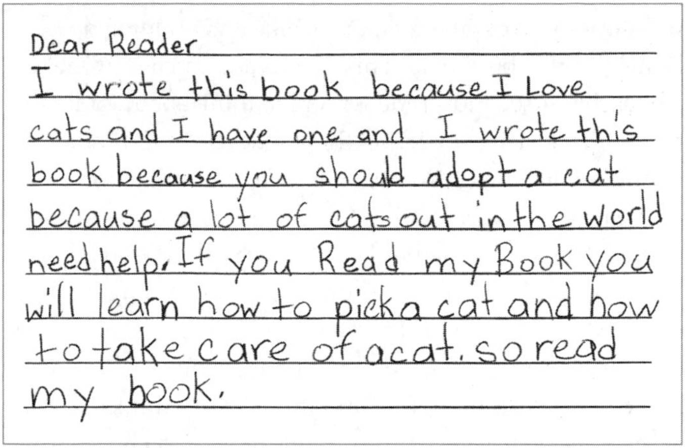

Dear Reader

I wrote this book because I Love cats and I have one and I wrote this book because you should adopt a cat because a lot of cats out in the world need help. If you Read my Book you will learn how to pick a cat and how to take care of a cat. so read my book.

FIG. 4.2 *Lissette's Introduction to Her Book about Cats*

structure that introductions can have. It might help to show writers that they can end their introductions by egging the reader on, saying something like, "Turn the page to get started!" or "Read on to find out all about karate!"

Informational writers end with a powerful conclusion, or "review," restating their most important ideas and saying again why this topic matters so much

Teaching young writers about endings can be some of the toughest work we do as writing teachers! It's likely we've spent days and days of minilessons trying to help our writers see how, ". . . and then we went home" is no way to end a powerful tale of longing for, and searching for, and at last finding the perfect Halloween costume, nor the way to end the woeful account of falling off one's bike and scraping up one's leg while one's brother and his friends are watching. One way we teach our second-grade writers to think about endings is that writers strive to leave their readers with a sense of closure—a feeling of "Ahhh" when they finish the story.

Readers of informational texts also long for closure. They want to feel like all the hard work they've done of reading to learn lots and lots of facts adds up to something—maybe something bigger than the facts themselves. If, up to this point in the unit, we haven't yet had a chance to teach our students that writers of informational texts think carefully about *why* their topic is important and try to change their readers hearts and minds—teaching conclusions is a great opportunity for this teaching and learning.

We can start by looking for informational texts in our classroom libraries that have conclusions for students to study. One favorite of mine comes from Jim Arnosky's *All About Owls* (1999). After describing how owls are beneficial by eating rodents, he ends the book with one last sentence that tells why owls are important, why we should care about them:

> And, of course, wherever they live, owls add a sense of mystery to the sounds and silence of the night.

Other conclusions "look forward," as in Seymour Simon's *Planets Around the Sun* (2002b):

> Far out in space, other planets circle other stars. But no one knows if any distant planets are like Earth. We still have much to learn about planets and stars.

Some writers use their conclusions to "check in" with their readers, to find out how their ideas about the topic are changing, like one second grader did in his book:

> What do you think about freshwater? *Your* opinion!!!! You could think freshwater is amazing and wonderful. You could also think it's greasy and nasty. I think it's beautiful, clean, and really fresh.

Writers choose a title by thinking, "What will get my readers interested in reading my book?"

Choosing a title is a process that varies greatly from writer to writer. Some writers seem to start with their titles in mind, letting the titles they choose shape the structure and content of their texts. Consider how choosing a title like *From Tadpoles to Frogs* or *Dangerous Animals* affects the way the entire book is laid out. For this reason, we may want to have students consider their titles early on in the unit, perhaps around the time they start creating their chapter titles.

Often, however, our writers will choose their titles toward the end of their writing process. One option is to teach them that writers can think, "What is the *most* important thing my reader will learn about my topic?" They might develop a title like, *It's a Good Thing There Are Insects* or *Fish Are Great Swimmers.* (See how Leigh tried this in Figure 4.3.) On the other hand, they may decide that the most important thing their readers will learn is that their topic is cool, or interesting, and thus go with simpler titles such as *Surprising Sharks* or *Amazing Bats.*

FIG. 4.3 *Leigh's Front Cover*

Some writers try to think up an interesting title that will attract and engage their readers. One approach to creating an interesting title is to use alliteration. We could show students the front covers of books such as *Busy, Buzzy Bees* or *Wiggling Worms at Work* and ask, "How could you use some words that start with the same letter as your topic to make your title fun to say?" Or, we could show student titles that use sound words, such as *Click! A Book About Cameras and Taking Pictures* or *Chomp! A Book About Sharks*, and say, "How could you use a sound word to get readers interested in your book?"

A quick perusal through our class' collection of nonfiction books will reveal that most nonfiction writers just keep it simple by naming their topics, such as *Penguins!* or *Ladybugs*. This is a fine choice to teach as well—texts with simple titles are not necessarily any less engaging!

Making It Clear—Teaching Conventions in Informational Writing

Second graders are beginning to uncover a growing curiosity for how language and punctuation works. They are interested in the "dot-dot-dots" of the ellipsis and the meaning of the "two-periods-on-top-of-each-other" colon. They notice patterns much more quickly than ever before, which helps them to secure spelling patterns, and they are able to begin generalizing and intuiting with greater accuracy where sentences end and which words require a capital letter.

I chose to include this focus on conventions here, toward the end of the book. However, this doesn't mean the only time we teach about conventions is at the end of a unit! Our teaching of writing conventions needs to happen on a daily and weekly basis—not just saved up until the final couple of days of a unit when we "edit" our writing. These conventions can be stressed during the revision and editing phase, but they should also be taught throughout this unit. As my colleague Shanna Schwartz wisely notes, "If we want to teach our writers to develop certain habits, then we have to teach those things *habitually*." When we plan any unit of study, we'll want to make sure that we include lots of teaching and reminding about conventions, using all of our teaching opportunities—minilessons, midworkshop teaching points, teaching shares, and small-group instruction.

However, we will most certainly be asking students to edit their work at the end of the unit to get it ready for publishing. After giving some ideas for ways to teach conventions throughout this unit, I'll offer a few tips for helping our students edit their writing more easily and efficiently.

Where to start? Which conventions should we teach?

Because our second graders' control of various writing conventions is as different from student to student as their fingerprints or their handwriting, there's no *one* way to suggest teaching conventions in this or any other unit. What I do suggest is that we start by studying our students' work and the Common Core State Standards. This will help us decide which conventions are worth focusing on with the whole class via minilessons and which conventions we'll address in specifically tailored small-group strategy lessons for students who need them most. See Figure 4.4 for one teacher's plan to support small groups across a variety of conventions in this unit.

During my experience working in classrooms across the country, I have found a few strategies that are taught over and over. Some of these lend themselves particularly well to an informational writing unit. The next section highlights several important conventions that second-grade teachers might consider teaching throughout the unit and then gives tips for

Monday	Tuesday	Wednesday	Thursday	Friday
Writing Conferences	Writing Conferences	Writing Conferences	Writing Conferences	Writing Conferences
Periods Group	Capitalization Group	Periods Group & Conferences	Capitalization Group	Conferences and/or other small groups
Sentence Combining	Periods Group & Conferences	Sentence Combining	Sentence Combining	Conferences and/or other small groups
Conferences and/or other small groups	Conferences and/or other small groups	Conferences and/or other small groups	Conferences and/or other small groups	Conferences and/or other small groups

FIG. 4.4 *One Teacher's Plan to Teach Conventions in Small Groups Across a Unit*

supporting students in using everything they've learned when they edit their writing at the end of the unit.

Teaching capitalization in an informational writing unit

Even though our second graders have been taught basic capitalization rules beginning in kindergarten, some have difficulty remembering to put capitals at the beginning of their sentences in their writing. And some young writers have developed a deeply entrenched habit of capitalizing letters randomly in the middle of words. The Common Core State Standards remind us that, in addition to correctly capitalizing the beginning of a sentence and people's names, second graders should be able to correctly capitalize names of geographic locations and names of products. What I've found is that many second-grade writers need better *habits* as they write—not another lecture on the "rules" of capitalization! It's best if they develop these habits on the run, learning to address capitalization as they write, thus ending the copious erasing that tends to happen at the end of each publishing cycle. We could pull together the writers in our class who need this reinforcement in a small group to practice one of the following strategies:

▶ **Writers constantly think as they write, "Does this word need a capital letter?"** We can model how writers quickly think to themselves when writing each and every word—does this word need a capital letter? Then we can coach our writers, whispering before they write each word, "Does that word need a capital letter?" (This coaching prompt extends beyond the first letter to the middles of words, too!) It's helpful to have a chart on capitalization in kid-friendly language to which you refer often during writing workshop and, in particular, while coaching.

▶ **Writers say their idea, write their idea, put a period, then . . . *capital*!** I like to teach this first as a chant, complete with motions to go along with it, "Say your idea! Write your idea! Period! *Capital*!" When we say, "Period!" we poke the air with our finger, and when we say, "Capital!" we reach our finger way up high to mimic the motion of starting a capital letter. After practicing the chant a few times, I ask students to add more to a chapter in their informational books and to use the chant to remember what to do next.

▶ **Writers put capitals at the beginning of important places and names.** Because of the emphasis on specialized vocabulary in informational writing, a unit of study on informational writing is an ideal opportunity to remind your writers to capitalize proper nouns. To do this, we might study a page of nonfiction text together and discuss which words the author has capitalized. It's helpful to make a chart with students that highlights the difference between common nouns and proper nouns. Then, help them apply this difference to their own informational writing by asking specific questions, "Brandon, your book is about dogs. Is *dog* a word that we should capitalize? What about *Saint Bernards*?"

▶ **Writers capitalize titles and headings.** The informational writing unit is a perfect opportunity to investigate capitalization in titles and headings. Young writers often need concrete and hands-on experiences to identify and explore new concepts. One teacher I know photocopied the front covers from several nonfiction texts the class had read and passed them out to writing partners. She gave each partnership two colored crayons—one red and one blue. "Circle the capital letters in red," she instructed. "Then circle the lowercase letters in blue. Talk with your partner about what you notice about which words have capital letters."

When the class reconvened, she asked the students to try to articulate which words in the titles were

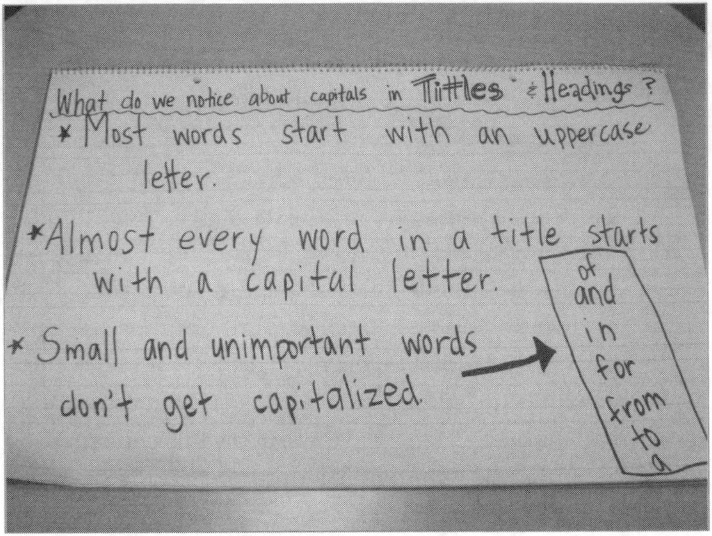

FIG. 4.5 *One class records their observations about capitalization.*

capitalized. One student put it this way, "It's like the big, long, important words in the title get a capital letter, and the little, short words—like *the* and *to*—don't get a capital letter." The teacher then made a chart with students that reflected their emerging understanding of the rules for capitalizing titles and headings. (See Figure 4.5.)

Teaching end punctuation in an informational writing unit

As noted with capitalization, second-grade writers often know that they *should* be putting end punctuation in their writing—they just aren't doing it consistently! We can help them become more consistent in this unit by keeping a laser-like focus on end punctuation and by studying the sentence variety that the best nonfiction can offer readers.

▶ **Writers say their idea, write their idea, then . . . period!** Alternately, we can tell our students that informational writers "Say a fact, write a fact . . . period!" We repeat this chant with motions—pointing to our mouths, writing in the air, and poking it enthusiastically when we get to the "period!" The key to getting writers into better habits here is to coach them *as* they write— adding all the periods after we've written a whole page not only isn't efficient, it isn't what real writers do at all! Here's how I coached one writer in a small strategy group after we practiced this chant several times:

M: Okay, Reina, say your first idea.

R: Second graders read short books and long books.

M: Now write your idea.

  (Reina writes while I look on.)

M: Now?

  (Reina writes a period.)

M: Nice! Now, say your next idea.

R: We read chapter books.

(I nod without a word as Reina begins writing the next sentence. When Reina gets to the last word of the sentence, I touch her lightly on the shoulder as she writes a period.)

When I coached Reina, I started by coaching her verbally with each part of the strategy, and then I gradually offered lighter and lighter prompts, such as using nonverbal cues like nodding or tapping her lightly on the shoulder, to help her internalize the strategy more and more deeply.

▶ **Informational writers don't just tell. They wonder and exclaim!** After a while, some information books can start to sound monotonous, with robotic recitals of fact after fact. If I notice writing that needs a bit more voice and sentence variety, I lean on conventions to help me accomplish this. I call writers together, asking them to bring their information books and say, "Writers, sometimes when we teach with our writing, we can get too caught up in telling everything we know—telling one fact, then another, then another. And we forget that informational writers don't just tell—they also wonder and exclaim!" I find it often helps to show writers an example from a mentor text to demonstrate this kind of writing. Next, I show writers an example from a mentor text, or perhaps my own writing, in which the author uses questions to say more, perhaps posing questions to readers or including some of his or her own questions. I pass out index cards with question marks and exclamation points on them. "Can you look at the punctuation mark you have in your hand? Now, look down at the chapter you're writing, and think, 'Can I add something I wonder or ask the reader a question? Can I exclaim over something—add a big feeling I have about the information on this page?' Then, turn and tell your partner what you could add." After partners talk for a few minutes, I have them switch index cards and ask them to

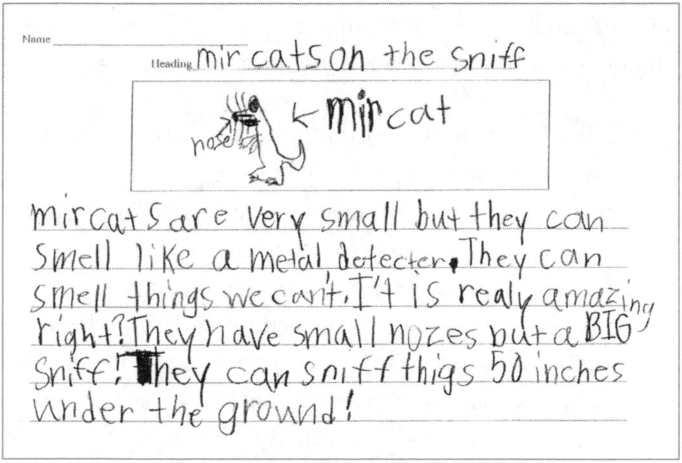

FIG. 4.6 *Brian uses a variety of end punctuation to get readers interested in his topic.*

think of more wonderings or exclamations. See how Brian used a variety of punctuation in his chapter about meerkats after this lesson. (See Figure 4.6.)

Teaching about commas in an informational writing unit

One of the notable features of informational writing is that writers tend to pack more information into each sentence. They tend to write sentences like, "Polar bears are covered with fur, which keeps them warm in the cold winters," or "A puppy is a young dog, just like a baby is a young person." Second graders can learn to write longer sentences that are lists or combine sentences to make their writing more engaging for their readers and to make their writing sound more like mentor informational texts. We can pull together a small group of second graders who are ready and try a few of these strategies:

- **Writers teach by making lists, separating each item with a comma.** Including lists can be an effective elaboration strategy for many young writers. The Common Core State Standards suggest that by the end of first grade, writers use commas to separate items in a series. It is fitting to remind your second graders of this convention as a way to support list-making. I often start by asking writers to reread a chapter from their informational book and put their finger on something in that chapter they know a lot about and about which they might make a list. I model first with my own writing, reading it aloud, and stopping after each sentence, saying, "Hmm . . . could I make a list about that? Could I make a list of kinds of running shoes? Or the different parks to run in in New York City?" I then help writers who need help finding possible opportunities for list-making in their own writing.

- **Writers make their sentences teach a lot by combining some sentences—using comma, *and*, or comma, *but*.** It helps for students to practice this together first in a shared text before trying it in their own writing. Tell students that writers try to pack more information into one sentence by using a comma and the word *and* or *but*. Then we can put these two choices on footlong sentence strips and reread the class text. As we do, we can place the sentence strip over the period in a sentence and think aloud, "Can we make this sentence even longer? Can we teach even more information about this?"

At the Bronx Community Charter School, second graders worked on a class book about *Food in Chinatown*. They revised a text that read:

> They sell many kinds of fruits and vegetables in Chinatown. Dragonfruit is pink and spiky. Bok choy has green leaves.

to read:

> Dragonfruit is pink and spiky, **but** it won't hurt you! Bok choy has green leaves, **and** it tastes like lettuce.

As students try extending and combining sentences, they often discover even more details to add to their writing.

▶ **Study examples of longer sentences with commas in mentor texts.** Young writers need not know what a clause is in order to write one! For writers who are ready to write more complex sentences, studying informational writing can be a great jumping-off point. We can pull these writers together to read longer mentor sentences that we've copied from nonfiction texts onto chart paper or sentence strips. Notice:

- The ways mentor writers conjoin ideas, identifying the words that are used often in these kinds of sentences—such as *when, during,* and *because.*
- Which part of the sentence is shorter and which part is longer.

- The kinds of punctuation used in these longer sentences—commas, dashes, or perhaps even colons.

Then invite students to try creating a few sentences for the shared text, using the structure of these sentences as mentors. At first, students may need a lot of teacher support to try this. I often start by writing an outline of the sentence, then invite the students to try saying the next part of the sentence. For example, when using the sentence from Seymour Simon's *Animals Nobody Loves* (2002a), "Cockroaches like the dark, so when you turn on the light in a roach-infested kitchen, they scurry off in all directions," I wrote this outline on the board:

Second graders like _____, so when _____, they will _____.

Katie came up with this sentence: "Second graders like recess, so when it's 12:00, they will run outside as fast as they can!"

Teaching strong word choice in an informational writing unit

Part of learning to write informational texts well is to learn to choose the best possible words to communicate what we are trying to teach. The words that informational writers use help readers not only to understand the information but also to navigate through the text. Strategies we teach our second graders to *read* informational texts well—such as paying attention to important terms and noticing transition words that show connections between pieces of information—often help us to teach our second graders to *write* informational texts well.

▶ **Writers choose the best way to teach important terms that the reader needs to know.** The Common Core State Standards refer to some terms used in an informational text as "domain-specific," that is, words and phrases that are specific to the topic and that are defined in the text. There are several ways information writers can define important terms, and studying mentor texts is often a helpful way to create a list of these ways. For example, writers can include a definition of important terms right in the text where the word appears. Often, they use commas to do this, pausing the sentence to tell the reader what a word means. Or, they might put important words in boldface and define them at the end of the book in a glossary. Writers might also provide the definitions of words in a text box on the page where the word first appears.

▶ **Writers use transition words to connect pieces of information.** Although the Common Core State Standards do not specifically mention use of transition words in informational texts until grade three, there is no reason not to teach our second graders words they can use to make connections between information and ideas. Information writers often use words such as *also, another, and, more,* or *but* to continue an idea or to introduce a different idea.

Fixing Up Our Writing for Readers—Editing in Informational Writing

Editing is a time that can feel shaky, even in the most experienced writing teachers' classrooms. One day our writing workshop can be humming along, with students busily writing and working away, and the next, it suddenly slams to a stop, with students unable to sustain the hard work of editing and the teacher feeling torn and harried, wanting to be everywhere and with every writer at once. Here are several things to keep in mind to help make the editing process go more smoothly:

▶ **Avoid asking students to edit for too many things.** Editing requires focused, reflective concentration. When we ask young writers to correct for too many things as they edit, this kind of concentration becomes very difficult to sustain. In my experience, the maximum number of conventions that second graders can edit for independently is around three or four. There may be students who can manage more, but generally each convention will require the student to read the entire text while really focusing on that convention. Rereading an informational book three times seems about the right number to provide a challenge while avoiding overwhelming the student.

▶ **Avoid asking students to edit for conventions they haven't yet mastered.** If I am a second-grade writer who doesn't yet completely understand what a sentence is, it's going to be difficult for me to accurately edit for end punctuation. It's important to be sure that we have provided sufficient instruction and practice with the conventions we want students editing for. Even with lots of instruction and practice, it's likely that the writers in our class vary greatly in their ability to correct a wide range of errors in their writing. Many teachers I work with solve this problem by creating several different editing checklists—some with more basic editing items, and some with more sophisticated editing items. They then give each student the checklist they'll be most successful with independently.

▶ **Do come well prepared on your Editing Day(s).** Because editing requires such sustained, reflective attention, and I know such attention can be difficult for some young writers to achieve, I plan carefully for the days that are designated for editing in my units. First, I make sure students realize that editing means reading and rereading our writing, thinking carefully about how we can make it easier to read. I create a tally system for students to track their rereading. Depending on the time of the year, I may ask students to read their writing two to three times on their own and then two to three times with a partner, making a tally mark each time they reread it to check for a different convention. I also make sure that I provide a clear checklist of next steps for students to independently follow while they wait for a teacher to support them with their editing work. This checklist might include working on creating a front cover, coloring illustrations in their texts, or making an "About the Author" or Dedication page.

Lucy Calkins was the first to remind us that our job as teachers is to "Teach the writer, not the writing" (2001b). That is to say that our best instruction does not focus on the narrow goal of improving one writing piece but, rather, reaches beyond this writing piece to transform the habits our writers have as they approach every piece of writing—be they habits of mind or habits of practice. The hope is that our instruction equips writers with new tools as well as the coaching they need to use those tools in a way that's automatic and instinctive. The complex tools of revising, punctuation, capitalization, and editing will surely not be completely grasped and internalized in one year's instruction. But through thoughtful assessment and systematic small-group coaching, we will begin to see second-grade writers developing stronger habits and greater proficiency as meaning makers.

CHAPTER FIVE

Celebrations and Beyond

Afternoon all of the hard work we have been immersed in during this unit, it's time to plan a celebration worthy of our efforts! Although a writing celebration needn't be an elaborate event, it's nice for some units to conclude with a more thoughtful commemoration. And this unit certainly lends itself to a wide variety of celebrations. This chapter offers some ideas for fun and meaningful ways to have students celebrate and reflect on the writing they've made in this unit.

We will also want to think of ways to maintain and extend the strategies that students have learned in this unit. Writing information well is a key skill that students will use as they progress through school, and the lessons they've learned in this unit will serve them well in future informational and essay writing. Therefore, this chapter also offers some ideas for ways to integrate more informational writing into our classrooms and to integrate the strategies that students have learned into future writing units.

Celebrating and Reflecting on Informational Writing

As we think about how to plan a celebration that reflects the work of our unit, we should think about varying the "where," "what," "how," and "with whom" of our celebration. The following is only a short list of possibilities:

> ▶ **Take our celebration to another classroom.** Students love the experience of being experts and teaching others. They could take their writing down to the first grade or kindergarten to teach them all they know about their topics. Or, they could take their writing to a fourth- or fifth-grade "buddy" and teach the big kids!

> ▶ **Take our celebration on the road.** Another way to celebrate this unit might be to think about places connected to the topics that many of our students taught about—perhaps the zoo, if many chose to write about animals, or the park, if many wrote about sports. Or, we might take students to a local university, explaining that this is where many people go to learn and teach, and have students read their pieces to each other outside on the university steps or in a library.

> ▶ **Share our writing through oral presentation.** It's quite natural to integrate an oral presentation into an informational writing unit. We can have students make a larger visual—such as a diagram on chart paper—to display during the presentation. Or students could write five important facts or chapter headings on an overhead

transparency to teach from. Or technology could be integrated by scanning in some of the students' drawings as slides for a PowerPoint-type presentation.

Reflecting on Our Writing

Just as important as celebrating students' finished writing pieces will be reflecting on what they've learned as writers in this unit. Second graders are at a crucial stage in their development of a writing identity. Every publishing cycle offers new opportunities for writers to synthesize new understandings about genre and writing process. In my own classroom, I always took the workshop time the day after any publishing celebration as a time to reflect on our progress as writers. This reflection can be done as a whole class, in partnerships, or individually.

▶ **Reflecting together as a class.** At the end of the unit, we can pull together all of our students on the rug with their writing folders. We can say, "When we get to the end of an important writing project, it's important to take time to think back over what we did. We can think about the parts that were hard and what helped us get through the hard parts. And we can think about the parts that were easy. We think about what we've learned about writing, so that it can help us the next time we have a writing project." Then we can ask students to spend a few minutes reading through all of the pages they made throughout the project. After talking to a partner for a few minutes, the class might embark on a discussion while the teacher charts their responses. The beginning of one class's very long reflection chart looked like this:

What helps us make great informational writing (or All-About books)?
- "You have to make it interesting for your reader. Put in comparisons or little jokes." Sam
- "Try to picture your topic in your mind." Layla
- "If you don't know what else to write, go to another page and come back to it." Keisha
- "Ask your reader a question to get them interested." Esteban

▶ **Reflecting in partnerships.** Second-grade writers can use their partners to help them reflect on the work they've done in the unit. Partners can interview each other, using questions such as:
- Why did you choose this topic?
- What was easy for you in this unit? Why? Show me in your writing.
- What was hard for you in this unit? Why? Show me in your writing.
- What new strategies helped you the most? Show me in your writing.

Then all the partnerships can gather back on the rug to share their partner's responses and how they were the same or different from their own responses. Partner reflections can be especially helpful for writers who might struggle with individual, written reflection.

▶ **Reflecting individually.** In my experience, second graders can produce meaningful written reflections on their work, but some may need significant support and practice at first. I've found that the most successful individual reflections often come after a whole-class discussion in which the teacher and students discuss the journey they took over the course of the unit and the strategies they learned. This reflection time can also be an opportunity for goal-setting, helping writers to use their reflections to think about future writing. (See the Appendix for an example.)

Looking Beyond the Informational Writing Unit

Now that our students are becoming more secure with the process of developing subtopics and writing information in ways that are clear and engaging, they're going to want to bring these new skills to bear in other ways. Here are a few ways to integrate structures and strategies from this unit throughout our school day, and throughout our school year:

▶ **Read aloud with writers' eyes.** As we continue to read aloud nonfiction books and articles, we should keep an eye on the author's structure and craft, in addition to the content our students are learning. During one read-aloud, we might read a few pages and, after discussing the content on the page, we might discuss how the author is trying to make the readers interested in the information, how we think the author wants us to feel about what we're learning, and how the author does that.

▶ **Offer lots of opportunities for informational writing.** The few days after or before a class trip offer great opportunities to have students use what they know about informational writing to make minibooks or chapters about their experiences and what they've learned. Encourage students to focus their topics, so that their pieces will be more clear and interesting, so that instead of the whole class writing "All About the Zoo" some students can write about "Tiger Country" and others "The Reptile Room," and so on. Writing during and after vacations is a great opportunity to offer a choice of informational writing. Students could teach others about an activity or place they visited over their vacations. Keeping our charts and mentor texts from the unit available will ensure that students more easily remember and use all of the rich strategies we taught during the unit.

▶ **Get specialist teachers involved.** The other teachers in our buildings often have only vague ideas about the curriculum we're teaching in our classrooms. The informational writing unit is a wonderful one to share with specialist teachers, to give them ideas of ways students could write about what they're learning in the arts or content areas. Think of all of the rich informational texts students could write—teaching about music, science, or even gym!

▶ **Make connections in other units.** On the face of it, it may seem like the skills and strategies learned in an informational writing unit may not transfer to other units. However, writers can use many of the skills they developed during informational writing in other units. For poetry, writers can practice using their senses, making comparisons, and thinking of numbers, names, shapes, and sizes that go with their topics. After an informational unit, students might return to personal narrative with a deeper sense of audience, rereading their stories, thinking, "What is this story *really* about? What do I want my reader to think or feel about this?" and to begin to add details, thoughts, and responses that angle their stories more. Second-grade writers could certainly try their hand at more literary nonfiction, perhaps during a unit of independent writing projects, when some students could study mentor texts and write various nonfiction structures—ABC books, narrative nonfiction (stories that teach), songs, and so on.

When I first began teaching writing workshop, I had a second grader named John B. John B. was the kind of kid who kept to himself. By that I mean he barely spoke a word. He lived with his dad, his twin brother, and his older brother who was currently in Juvenile Hall. John B. was a second grader who almost never smiled, and he was a second grader who drew guns. Lots of guns. And flying. His pictures had lots of flying. As much as I would insist he try to find a small moment from his life, John B. would draw flying, guns, fire, and sometimes bad guys. When I'd try to talk to him about his stories, about his life, he maintained a hard and stubborn silence, kept his eyes intently on his paper, waiting me out. And when I'd finally give him one last encouraging compliment and walk away, he wouldn't respond; he'd simply return to drawing guns, and fire, and bad guys.

It stayed pretty much the same all fall, until one day in winter, when we started our informational writing unit, I walked over to John B.'s desk and noticed he was making a new kind of drawing. This one had a figure with its feet firmly on the ground, a figure that actually resembled John B. And he had drawn a long line across the page to another figure, on which he was drawing small zigzags. I sat down.

"Hi, John," I started. "What are you teaching about?"

John looked up at me warily. He looked down at his paper. I waited. After a minute or so, he finally whispered, "It's Spooky."

At first, I misunderstood, thinking we were back to bad guys and guns.

"You're teaching about something spooky?" I asked.

He shook his head and put his finger on the page. "My dog is Spooky," he said, keeping his eyes in his lap.

"Oh wow," I nodded, leaning forward to get a better look at his paper. This was the most complete sentence he'd uttered since I'd met him. "Your dog's name is Spooky?"

"He's brown. He's a Lab," John B. said, picking up his pencil and resuming drawing the spikes in Spooky's fur, still not making eye contact. "He sleeps with me at night."

I nodded and thought about this for a moment.

"John? Would you be willing to teach the class about Spooky? You must know so much—like about what he eats, and what he does. Do you think you could write a whole book about Spooky and other dogs like him?"

Later that week, John B. stood at the front of the classroom holding a large drawing of a dog. He pointed to the dog and read the words he'd written below his drawing:

Dogs have two eyes. Dogs have four legs and they have fur. My dog has brown fur, but some dogs have white and black and yellow. Dogs have a tongue and they lick you. They have a tail and they wag it when they are happy to see you. Dogs are warm. They have a heart. When they lay next to you at night, you can feel the heart beating.

In her book, *Living Between the Lines,* Lucy Calkins observed, "If we adults listen and watch closely, our children will invite us to share their worlds and their ways of living in the world" (1991). On that winter day, the class and I were finally offered a precious invitation into the world of John B. On the days after that, we became more and more closely knit together as we taught each other and shared our passions. We learned about Tara's brother's learning disability and about Dashawn's zeal for recycling. Donald made us think twice about eating meat in his informational book about vegetarianism, while Justin made us roll with laughter over the antics of baby brothers.

What I discovered then, and long for all teachers to discover, is this: the tools we give writers that enable them to teach with clarity and engagement are more than just tools for writing well—they are tools for *living* well. If we care to live in a world whose citizens have the power and the sense of duty to enrich the world with their energy and ideas, then we must create classrooms that channel and champion a seven-year-old's natural spirit of inquisitiveness and un-restrained enthusiasm. This kind of learning, this kind of living, is possible for all of our students, no matter their struggles. Our greatest hope is that by encouraging students to bring in the "stuff" of their lives and to pursue and write about their passions, our students will develop the language and tools they'll need to inform and influence the world's hearts and minds and to author a life imbued with passion and a wide-eyed sense of discovery.

WORKS CITED

Arnosky, Jim. 1999. *All About Owls*. New York: Scholastic.

Beers, Kylene. 2003. *When Kids Can't Read, What Teachers Can Do: A Guide for Teachers 6–12.* Portsmouth, NH: Heinemann.

Bees! Time for Kids Series. 2005. New York: HarperCollins.

Calkins, Lucy. 2001a. *The Art of Teaching Reading*. Boston: Allyn and Bacon.

———. 2001b. *The Art of Teaching Writing.* Portsmouth, NH: Heinemann.

———. 1991. *Living Between the Lines*. Portsmouth, NH: Heinemann.

Calkins, Lucy, and Abby Oxenhorn. 2003. *Small Moments: Personal Narrative Writing*. Portsmouth, NH: Heinemann.

Calkins, Lucy, and Laurie Pessah. 2003. *Nonfiction Writing: Procedures and Reports.* Portsmouth, NH: Heinemann.

Calkins, Lucy, and Kathleen Tolan. 2009. *Navigating Nonfiction, Volume One, Units of Study for Teaching Reading, Grades 3–5.* Portsmouth, NH: Heinemann.

Dussling, Jennifer. 1998. *Bugs! Bugs! Bugs!* New York: DK Children.

Fountas, Irene C., Andrea McCarrier, and Gay Su Pinnell. 1999. *Interactive Writing: How Language and Literacy Come Together, K–2.* Portsmouth, NH: Heinemann.

Freedman, Russell. 2004. Interview with Laura Robb. *Nonfiction Writing From the Inside Out.* New York: Scholastic.

National Governors Association Center for Best Practices and Council of Chief State School Officers. 2010. *Common Core State Standards for English Language Arts.* Available at: www.corestandards.org/assets/CCSSI_ELA%20Standards.pdf. Accessed on October 4, 2011.

Seymour, Simon. 2002a. *Animals Nobody Loves.* San Francisco: Chronicle Books.

———. 2002b. *Planets Around the Sun.* San Francisco: Chronicle Books.

Vygotsky, Lev. 1978. *Mind in Society: Development of Higher Psychological Processes.* Cambridge: Harvard University Press.

Reflection: How am I getting better at teaching with my writing?		
	This was easy for me . . .	This was hard for me . . .
I chose a topic that I know a lot about.		
I organized my teaching into chapters for my table of contents.		
I tried to squeeze my brain and teach even more about my topic by using my senses.		
I tried to squeeze my brain and teach even more about my topic by picturing my topic in my mind.		
I tried to squeeze my brain and say even more about my topic by using comparisons.		
I made my pictures teach even more by adding more details and more words.		
I made paper choices to make my teaching more interesting and clear for my reader.		
I tried to change my readers' hearts and minds about my topic.		
I made my writing easy to read for my reader by fixing up my capitalization, spelling, and punctuation.		

In this unit I am proud of _____

_____

_____

My next goals are _____

_____

_____

Consider these other books in the

A QUICK GUIDE TO
Teaching Second-Grade Writers with Units of Study
LUCY CALKINS

Responding to the developmental and educational needs of second-grade writers, Lucy Calkins chronicles a curricular calendar that will help teachers increase the volume of student writing; encourage students to lift the level of their writing by reviewing, rethinking, and rewriting their work; and empower students to write with greater independence.

A QUICK GUIDE TO
Teaching Persuasive Writing, K–2
SARAH PICARD TAYLOR

Children have voices that need to be heard and ideas that need to be understood. Building on this premise, Sarah describes why you should try a persuasive writing unit of study, describes two units of study for the primary classroom, and lists tips and ideas for helping students get their persuasive writing out into the world.

Pocket-sized professional development on topics of interest to you.